ACKNOWLEDGEMENTS

A few people you cannot thank enough. Mark Krebs, Denny Larr Taylor, George Stephenson and John Walker each took on this project in a very personal way. Their extraordinary enthusiasm and diverse talents were offered generously and gratefully accepted.

The assistance of Ted Amussen, Jeanne Viner, Kay Chabot, Marlow Cook, Jeri Charles, Irmy Gray, Orval Hansen, Gary Livak, Howard Means, Sherrie Sandy and Dell Smith was also invaluable.

We would like to thank Tom and Kathleen Bagby, Perry Fisher, Jack and Carolyn Fleming, Janice Frey, Georgia Grant, Roger and Teel Grant, Dr. Tom Hegarty, John Hartmann, T. Iglehart, Dr. Tom Kangur, Phil Kimble, Dave Kudravetz, Barbara Grant Llewellyn, Jack Limpert, Kathleen Lunsford, Leo Mullen, Linda Otto, George Patten, Jerry Saffer, John Stalfort, Merry Thomasson, Holly Townsend, and Webb & Athey Advertising and Public Relations.

Special thanks to Anheuser-Busch Companies, Inc., Standard Oil Company (Indiana), Merrill Lynch and Co. Inc., International Telephone and Telegraph, Inc. and Martin Marietta Corporation, whose generous gift of books to the United States Government helped make this book possible.

Producer: Frank L. Thomasson III

Designer: John F. Grant

Research: Josephine Gibson, Fran Maclean

Editorial and Production Assistant: Jim Gibson

Project Co-ordinator: Mary Lynn Davis

Marketing Consultant: Michael P. Gleason

Page 50. From "Washington Monument at Night" in SLABS OF THE SUNBURNT WEST by Carl Sandburg, copyright 1922 by Harcourt Brace Jovanovich, Inc., renewed 1950 by Carl Sandburg. Reprinted by permission of the publisher.

Page 88. From "Look, stranger, on this island now" of W. H. AUDEN: COLLECTED POEMS, by W. H. Auden, edited by Edward Mendelson, copyright 1937 by Random House, Inc. Reprinted by permission of the publisher.

Library of Congress Catalog Number: 81-69086
Hardcover ISBN: 0-934738-02-5
Printed in U.S.A. by Stephenson, Inc., Alexandria, Virginia.
Published in 1981 by Thomasson-Grant Publishing, Inc.
Formerly Upland Publishing Inc.
2250 Old Ivy Road, Charlottesville, Virginia 22901.
(804) 977-1780

THOMASSON-GRANT

WASHINGTON

**THE
CAPITAL**

PHOTOGRAPHY
BY ROBERT LLEWELLYN

FOREWORD
BY CLEMENT E. CONGER

The city clung tenaciously to the steep jungle ridge, its art and religion mysteriously tied to far-off lands and lotus flowers, its stepped pyramids built to view the world across the broad plains of southern Mexico. The people called the place Palenque, a borrowed name; and with its temples of power and arts of gentleness, Palenque became the golden expression of the Mayan empire.

The explorers have been there, mindful searchers seeking among the vine and root for the footprints of a culture's passage on this Earth. Stone back on stone, the restorations bring back a people who survive in no form yet leave their spirit with us in each temple, each pyramid, each word carved upon the wall.

And Washington — another borrowed name, capital of a new civilization — what would be left of you? What temples, what palaces and cathedrals, what inscriptions along the Potomac — what would the explorers of the future build back to tell their own unborn what people we were, what we loved and longed for in this America.

ROBERT LLEWELLYN
1981

FOREWORD

In ancient Babylon, Persepolis, Luxor, Athens, Rome, Anghor Vat, and Machu Picchu, great men had great visions for the buildings that were to represent their cultures. Knowing that their cities and monuments would long outlast them, they employed the leading architects and builders of their times to plan and raise the public structures, in the process inspiring private buildings of force and grace. Far newer, Washington is still such a city — timeless, born of extraordinary vision.

On July 9, 1790, America's founding fathers created the new Capital City, borrowing an area ten miles square from Maryland and Virginia. Major Pierre-Charles L'Enfant, a French engineer, was commissioned to lay out this new American city. Over an expansive grid of lettered and numbered streets he superimposed a baroque scheme of radiating avenues. At the hub of this ambitious plan lay the site of the Capitol itself. L'Enfant, who remembered troubled times in Paris, placed traffic circles at outlying points to facilitate the deployment of artillery. Never used for this purpose, the circles now serve as sites for fountains, monuments, or statuary.

To locate the finest architectural talent for the Capitol and President's house, Thomas Jefferson, then Secretary of State, suggested open competitions. Among the unselected entries for the design of the President's house was Jefferson's own, submitted anonymously. Most of these architects looked back to the foundations of democracy for their inspiration, drawing upon the classical designs of the public buildings of ancient Greece and Rome.

In the decades which followed the completion of these two main structures, Washington began to fulfill its founders' visions. Its wide avenues, classical architecture, and extensive parks came to life even as the city exploded outward into the surrounding countryside to become a place that L'Enfant or Jefferson would recognize only with the greatest of effort. Yet as substantial as the City of Washington seems today, as firmly founded as it seems to be upon the map of the world, it sits — as the great world capitals that preceded it did — amidst unknowable forces of history.

What will be here in 2,000 years? In 5,000 years? Will new cities be layered on top of this one? Will Washington endure as Damascus in Syria — the oldest surviving national capital — has done; or will the tidal Potomac River rise with melting glaciers to submerge the city we know today?

Let us dream great visions like our founding fathers. Let us hope that Washington will survive throughout the ages — that its principal structures, like the Parthenon in Athens and the Pantheon in Rome, will not only still be standing, but will continue to be used, enjoyed, and admired as they are now.

These photographs of the capital of the New World show not only the Washington of today, but the essential Washington that may remain throughout eternal tomorrows.

CLEMENT E. CONGER

The Curator
The White House
and
Diplomatic Reception Rooms
Department of State

October, 1981

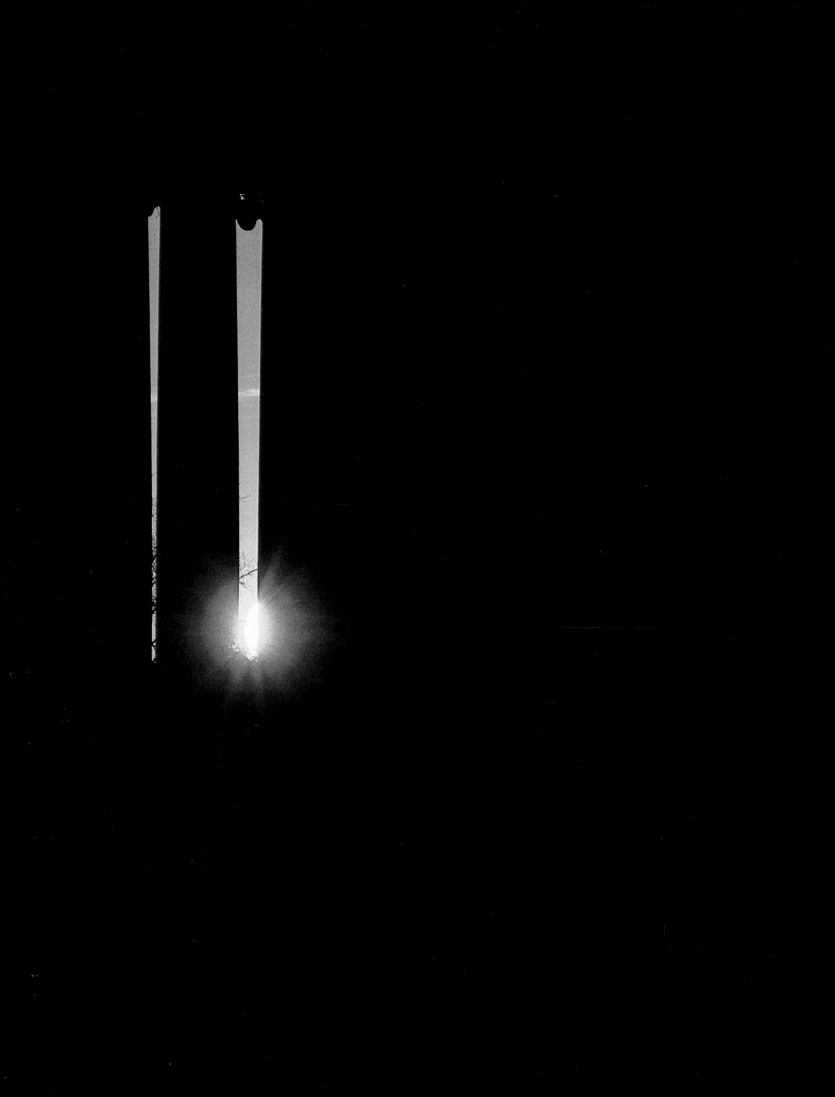

REGAIN THEREFORE YOUR OLD SPIRITS,
FOR RETURN I WILL NOT UNTIL
I HAVE FOUND THE PATAWOMECK.

Captain John Smith to his crew.

LAWS AND INSTITUTIONS MUST GO HAND IN HAND

WITH THE PROGRESS OF THE HUMAN MIND.

AS THAT BECOMES MORE DEVELOPED,

MORE ENLIGHTENED, AS NEW DISCOVERIES ARE MADE...

INSTITUTIONS MUST ADVANCE ALSO TO KEEP PACE WITH THE TIMES.

Thomas Jefferson

WE HEAR NOT THE AIRY FOOTSTEPS
OF THE STRANGE THINGS THAT ALMOST HAPPEN.

Nathaniel Hawthorne

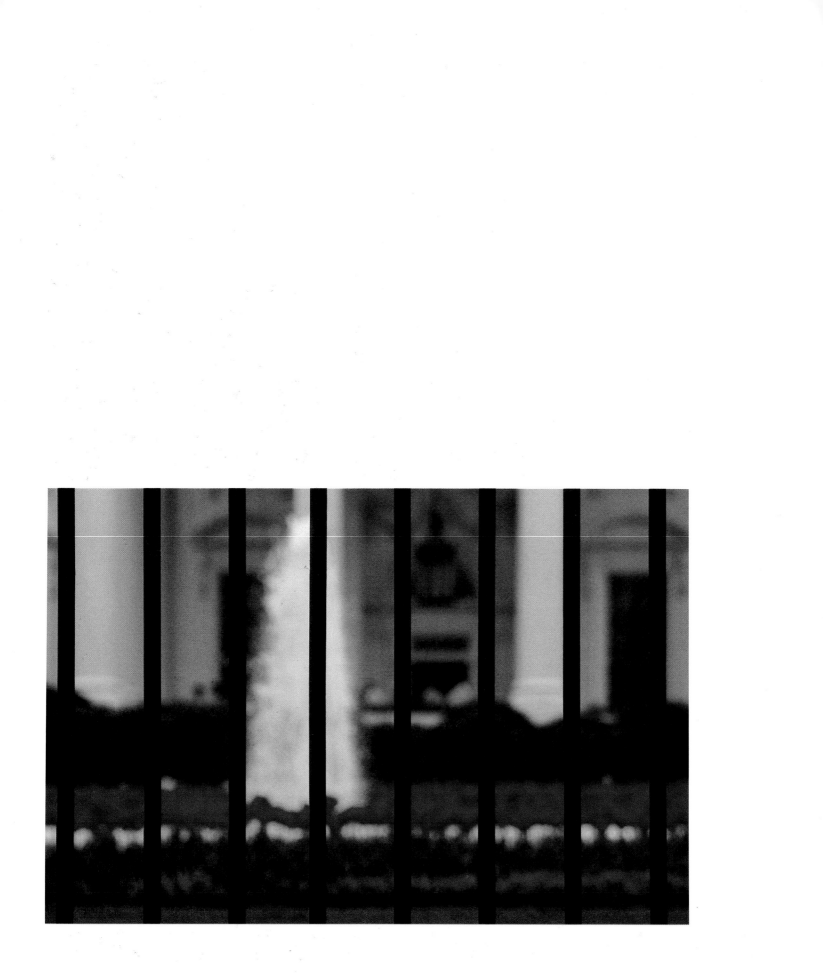

THIS IS THE LONELIEST PLACE IN THE WORLD.

William Howard Taft

BUT SUCH IS THE IRRESISTIBLE NATURE OF TRUTH,

THAT ALL IT ASKS, AND ALL IT WANTS,

IS THE LIBERTY OF APPEARING.

Thomas Paine

WHEREVER THE AMERICAN CITIZEN MAY BE
A STRANGER, HE IS AT HOME HERE.

Frederick Douglass

THE STONE GOES STRAIGHT.

A LEAN SWIMMER DIVES INTO NIGHT SKY,

INTO HALF-MOON MIST.

Carl Sandburg

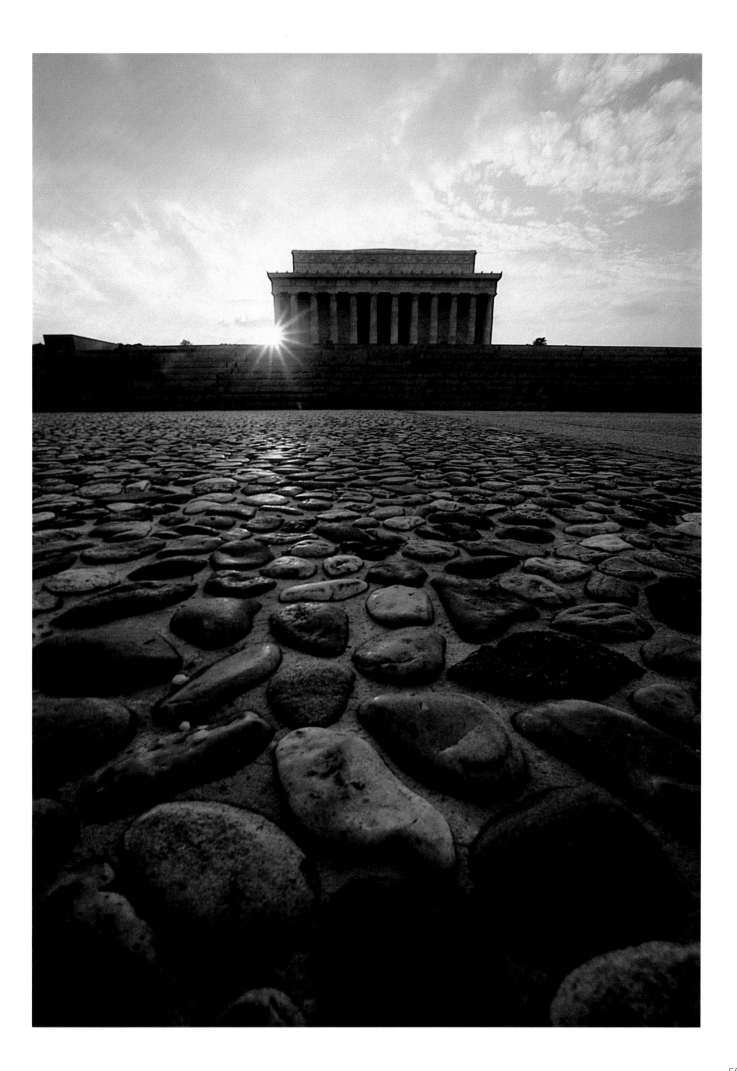

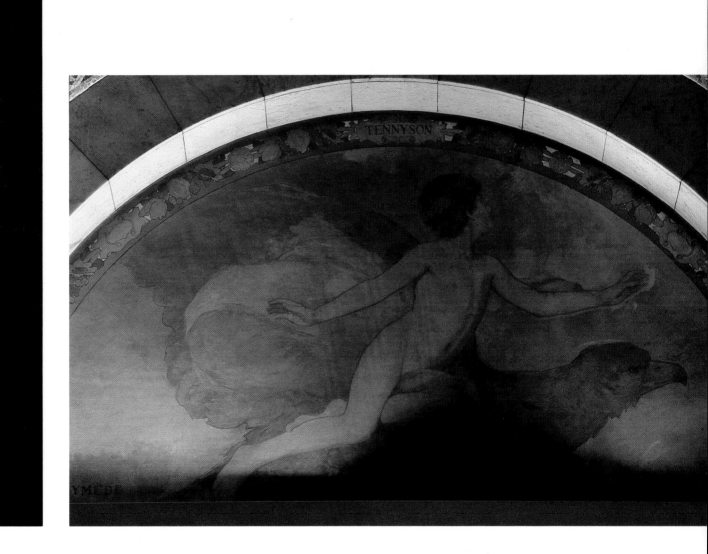

FLUSHED GANYMEDE, HIS ROSY THIGH
HALF-BURIED IN THE EAGLE'S DOWN,
SOLE AS A FLYING STAR SHOT THRO' THE SKY
ABOVE THE PILLAR'D TOWN.

Alfred, Lord Tennyson

ART COMES TO YOU PROPOSING FRANKLY TO GIVE NOTHING

BUT THE HIGHEST QUALITY TO YOUR MOMENTS AS THEY PASS.

Walter Pater

COURAGE IS THE PRICE THAT LIFE EXACTS

FOR GRANTING PEACE.

THE SOUL THAT KNOWS IT NOT,

KNOWS NO RELEASE FROM LITTLE THINGS.

Amelia Earhart Putnam

...JOY AND AMAZEMENT

AT THE BEAUTY AND GRANDEUR OF THIS WORLD

OF WHICH MAN CAN JUST FORM A FAINT NOTION.

Albert Einstein

CATHEDRALS,

LUXURY LINERS LADEN WITH SOULS,

HOLDING TO THE EAST THEIR HULLS OF STONE.

W. H. Auden

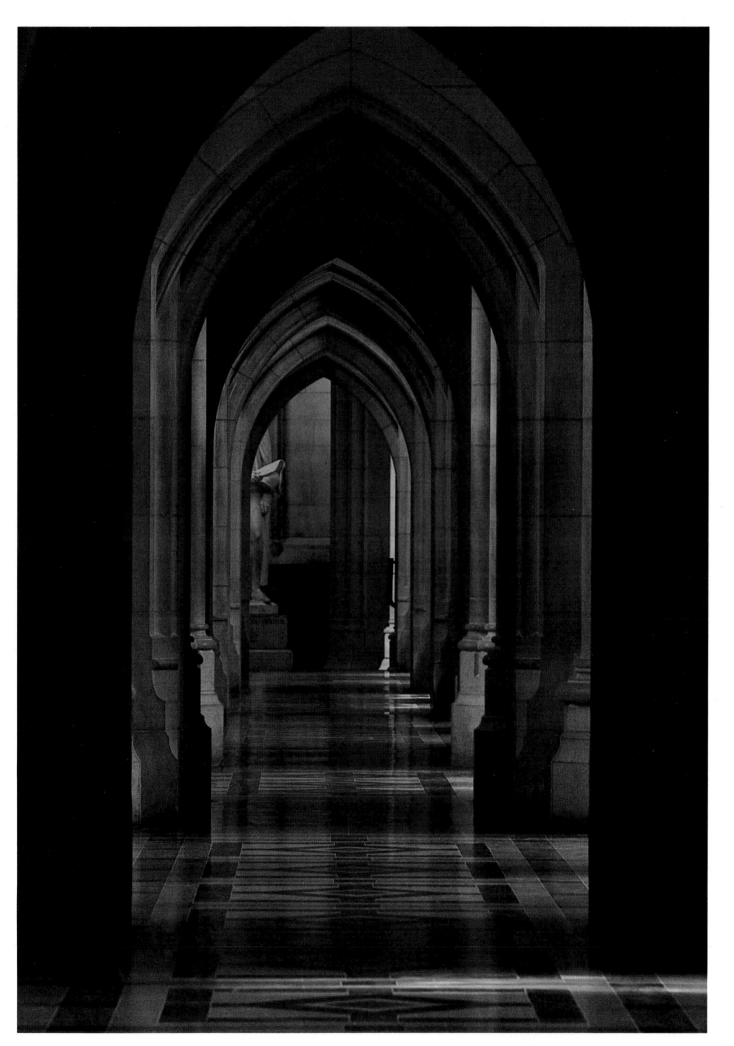

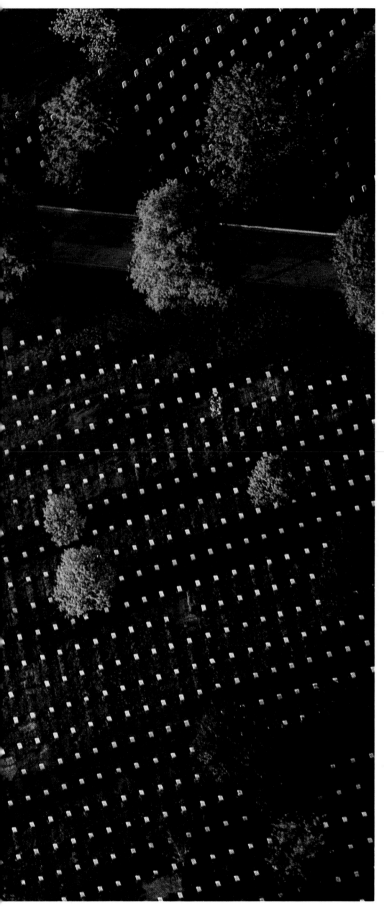

I THINK THE SLAIN

CARE LITTLE IF THEY SLEEP OR RISE AGAIN

AND WE, THE LIVING, WHEREFORE SHOULD WE ACHE

WITH COUNTING ALL OUR LOST ONES?

Aeschylus

MAY THE SPIRIT WHICH ANIMATED
THE GREAT FOUNDER OF THIS CITY,
DESCEND TO FUTURE GENERATIONS.

John Adams

THE PHOTOGRAPHS

1

Base of fluted pillar, Supreme Court Building. Many architects for Washington's public buildings looked to the temples of Ancient Greece and Rome for inspiration. They believed the pure, powerful lines of classical architecture best symbolized the concepts of a republican democracy.

2-3

Curving flow of traffic as it enters the Capital from Memorial Bridge.

4-5

Navy-Marine Memorial. This memorial on the banks of the Potomac commemorates the "long and hazardous voyages of the naval and merchant seamen who made the ocean safe for commerce and spread civilization over the earth." The tulips are just a few of the thousands of spring flowers that bloom in Washington as a result of Lady Bird Johnson's "Make America Beautiful" campaign.

8

Corner of the Jefferson Memorial. Adjoining the tidal basin and surrounded by flowering cherry trees, the Jefferson Memorial was built on land reclaimed from the Potomac River.

10

The Lincoln Memorial, the Washington Monument and the Capitol from Arlington Cemetery. Nowhere else is it more evident that the planners and architects of the nation's capital "borrowed" from many styles. The Lincoln Memorial is patterned after the Grecian Parthenon, the design of the Washington Monument is based on Egyptian obelisks, while the dome of the Capitol itself resembles that of St. Paul's Cathedral in London, designed by Sir Christopher Wren.

12-13

The Jefferson Memorial. It is said that sculptor Rudulph Evans opened his door to the postman one day, studied him carefully for several minutes and then invited him to pose for the Jefferson Memorial statue. The 19½-foot cast bronze figure stands on a six-foot black marble base under a dome similar to the one designed by Jefferson for his home, Monticello. The statue portrays Jefferson speaking to the Continental Congress, wearing the great-coat presented to him by General Thaddeus Kosciusko, who helped the Americans win the Revolutionary War.

14-15

The Potomac River.

17

Marigolds, cannas and the Capitol Building.

18

Old Senate Office Building. As the country grew, so did its government. The Old Senate Office Building, named after Senator Richard B. Russell, has been in use since 1909, when the legislative branch outgrew its office space in the Capitol. The facade is modeled after the East Front of The Louvre in Paris.

19

West Front of the Capitol from the terraces. The sandstone walls of the West Front remain the only walls of the original Capitol building that have not been replaced. Although in recent history, inaugurations have been held on the East Front, President Ronald Reagan chose to break with tradition and hold his inauguration ceremonies on these steps.

20

Peace Monument, West Capitol Grounds. Franklin Simmons' Italian marble sculpture symbolizes America weeping on the shoulder of History for the Navy men lost at sea during the Civil War. These figures demonstrate the continued influence of the classic style in the late nineteenth century.

21

Lincoln Statue in the Rotunda of the Capitol. Each of the 50 states is allowed to place statues of two of its distinguished citizens in the halls of the Capitol. Many of these can be found in Statuary Hall and the Rotunda. The Rotunda, the Capitol's great central room, is 180 feet high but only 97 feet across. It is topped by a massive cast iron dome weighing approximately nine million pounds. The coffering on the sides of the dome is a Roman construction technique that adds strength while keeping weight to a minimum.

22

Bronze railings, Capitol Building. Constantino Brumidi, the interior designer for the Capitol, designed these railings for the four stairways used exclusively by senators and representatives.

23

Senate Lobby. In this richly detailed private room just off the Senate Chamber, staffers whisper messages and receive instructions from their legislators.

24

Statue of Freedom atop the Capitol dome. The 19-foot female figure designed by Thomas Crawford to symbolize Freedom, was mounted on the Capitol dome in December 1863. The figure holds a sheathed sword in her right hand and a shield and a wreath in her left. An eagle's head and tail feathers in Freedom's headdress represent native North Americans. Although called "Freedom," the bronze casting was, ironically, made in nearby Maryland by slaves.

25

Relief on Rotunda pediment. Titled "Genius of America," John Quincy Adams championed this sculpture hoping to convey the concept that the Country (middle figure) may Hope (figure on the right) for success as long as it pursues Justice (figure on the left). The flag at half-staff honors World War II five-star General Omar Bradley.

26-27

The Capitol from the West Terrace. The grounds and terraces immediately surrounding the Capitol remain today much as Frederick Law Olmsted, renowned American landscape architect, planned them at the turn of the century. The Capitol, like much of the city, is surrounded by trees that are lush and dense in the summer, and a tangled web of branches through which to view the seat of power in winter.

28-29

White House, North Portico. The original design of the President's House by James Hoban, was inspired by the design of Leinster House, a gentleman's home in Dublin, Ireland. After the fire set by the British in 1814, the mansion was painted white for the first time to cover the burn marks. Although it was a white house, it did not become known as the White House until the presidency of Theodore Roosevelt. The North Portico, designed by Benjamin Latrobe, was added to the original building in 1829.

30

White House grounds. Fenced to assist in maintaining security of the White House, the 18-acre park surrounding the Executive Mansion provides an oasis of quiet for the president's home and office.

31

White House, South Portico. Other than the repairs required by the fire of 1814, there have been two major renovations of the executive mansion. In 1902, a complete redecoration restored the White House interior to its original, more classic style. The second-floor balcony was added at the request of Harry Truman because he liked to sit in the open air.

32

White House, East Room. Used for the most gala events — concerts, receptions, weddings and dances — the room has also been used for religious services and has been the site of many solemn historic events. The funerals of the presidents who died during their terms of office have also been held here.

33

Vermeil pitcher. One of a pair of matching gilded silver pitchers by nineteenth-century British silversmith, Paul Storr, that grace a mantle-piece in the East Room.

33

Painting of George Washington by Gilbert Stuart in the East Room.

34

The Oval Office. Each occupant of the Oval Office can choose from an extensive collection of historic furniture for the decoration of the White House, including the Oval Office. Some presidents use this formal office full time; others prefer to do most of their work in a small study nearby.

35

Window of the Oval Office. This is the window from which the president views the world. The Oval Office is located in a complex of offices known as the West Wing, lying between the White House and the Executive Office Building. It is directly connected to the White House.

36-37

Looking across the Ellipse toward the Potomac River. Pierre L'Enfant, in his plan for the City of Washington, drew a line down the Mall from the Capitol, and another line southward from the President's House to the river. He designated the point at the intersection of these axes as the site of a monument to George Washington. Unfortunately this spot had been the bed of the Tiber River and was considered too marshy to support the weight of the monument that was planned. The monument was, therefore, relocated several hundred feet away from the original site.

38, 39

The Executive Office Building. President Eisenhower wanted to tear it down; Hoover made plans to cover its baroque facade with a copy of the Treasury Building face. Truman didn't want to tear it down because, as he said, "I think it's the greatest monstrosity in America." Arthur Keyes, an architect, said, "It's a high water mark in low taste, but I love it." In attempting to describe the building's architectural heritage, it has been said that it is an "adaptation of nineteenth century French impressions of Italian attempts to imitate Greek classicism." Others simply characterized it as "Baroquerie gone frantic." The controversy over what to do with the old "gray lady" was finally decided by President John Kennedy, who, at the urging of William Walton, head of Washington's Fine Arts Commission, decreed that the building, formerly occupied by the State, War and Navy Departments, would be completely renovated.

40-41

The Supreme Court Building. From the early days of the republic the Supreme Court had been housed in the Capitol. It was not until 1935 that the Court moved into its own "palace of justice," designed by Cass Gilbert. Designed in the classical mode, the building is in the form of a central temple with a wing on each side, and stands behind a large decorative plaza.

42

Base of flag pole, Supreme Court Building.

43

Old Supreme Court Room in the Capitol. In the mid-1970s this room was restored to the way it looked in 1860 when it housed the Supreme Court.

44, 45, 46-47

The Washington Monument. Colorful umbrellas raised above the thronging visitors signal positions of tour guides. The Mall is a magnet for tourists because of the many museums located around its edges. In addition, there are many events presented on the Mall itself, such as an annual kite-flying contest, the Folklife Festival and elaborate Fourth of July fireworks displays. Inside the 555-foot shaft, which is the tallest structure in Washington, a high-speed elevator takes visitors to the look out station.

48

West facade of the Commerce Building. At the time it was built in the early 1900s, this building was part of the grand design for a "Federal Triangle" to house much of the government bureaucracy. It was planned as a single unified development. The buildings now occupy the triangular area bounded by Constitution Avenue, Pennsylvania Avenue and Fifteenth Street. They replaced a delapidated area of tenements, brothels and light industry. The Federal Triangle project was outgrown by the time most of it was built and the project was never really completed.

49

The Temples of Washington. The Lincoln Memorial, the Washington Monument and the Capitol—some of the majestic beauty L'Enfant envisioned when he planned Washington as the capital city for a new country.

50

The Washington Monument from the ground.

52-53, 54, 55

The Lincoln Memorial. Daniel Chester French, who designed the statue for the Lincoln Memorial, wanted it to be a relaxed figure, yet one that would portray Lincoln as a mighty and fearless man. He felt the hands held the answer to giving the statue the "calm of the best Greeks" while still retaining the intense personality of the subject. The Smithsonian Institution had plaster casts of Lincoln's hands, made the day he learned of his nomination for President. The cast of Lincoln's left hand was what French needed, but the other cast did not seem right, possibly because at the time the cast was made the right hand was swollen from so many congratulatory handshakes that day. The answer to securing a suitable model for the right hand, French decided, was to have a casting made of his own hand in the position he needed for the statue.

56-57

Memorial Bridge from the cornice of the Lincoln Memorial. Spotlights surrounding the memorial in January 1981 celebrate the return of the 52 American hostages from their imprisonment in Iran.

59

Cherry Blossoms. Soon after her husband became president, Mrs. William Howard Taft expressed an interest in planting Japanese Cherry Trees in Washington. Three years later the City of Tokyo sent 3,000 cuttings of a number of different varieties of cherry trees. In the 1940s, the original trees in Tokyo died, and in 1952, our nation returned the favor by sending cuttings from the Washington trees to replace them.

60

The Jefferson Memorial. The relief on the pediment of the memorial sets the scene for the statue inside. It shows Jefferson standing before the committee appointed by the Continental Congress to write the Declaration of Independence.

61

The Jefferson Memorial.

62-63

The Jefferson Memorial on the Tidal Basin. This memorial was designed by John Russell Pope using many of Jefferson's favorite architectural designs. It was dedicated on the 200th anniversary of Jefferson's birth by President Franklin D. Roosevelt.

64

Bust of Thomas Jefferson on the Great Staircase in the Library of Congress. For nearly 100 years the Library of Congress was housed in the Capitol until it moved to its own building in 1897. When the British burned the Capitol in 1814, the Library's meager collection was destroyed. Noting the situation, Jefferson wrote a letter to Congress: "You know my collection. I have been fifty years making it, and have spared no pains, opportunity, or expense to make it what it now is..." Congress offered $23,950 and the Jefferson library became the Library of Congress. Unfortunately another fire destroyed all but 2,000 volumes of the Jefferson library. These books are now housed in the Rare Book Room, along with the original of the letter with his offer.

65

Painting on the Walls of the Library of Congress. In "Palace of Art" Tennyson describes, among the other paintings that decorate the palace's walls, one of Ganymede borne aloft by an eagle. The story is that Jupiter came to earth in the form of an eagle to select a successor to Hebe, the cupbearer to the Gods. Flying over Mount Ida, he saw the Trojan prince Ganymede and carried him off to Mount Olympus.

66-67

The Library of Congress Reading Room. Although the library does not allow its books to be removed from the building by the general public, anyone may consult them in the reading room.

68

Dome of the Library of Congress Reading Room.

69

Neptune Fountain on the retaining wall at the Library of Congress. This detail shows a bronze sea nymph sitting astride a sea horse rising out of the water. The figure was sculpted by R. Hinton Perry.

70-71

East Building of the National Gallery of Art. Designed by I.M. Pei, this trapizoidal addition to the National Gallery was built on one of the last portions of the Mall available for development. Although it was built primarily to provide additional office space, it holds many permanent and short-term exhibits.

72-73

Hirshhorn Museum of Modern Art. When Joseph Hirshhorn donated his collection of 4,800 paintings and 1,500 sculptures to the United States, he insisted they be housed in a thoroughly modern building. In October 1974, the circular, concrete structure, with an outdoor sunken sculpture garden, took its place among the predominantly classical architecture of the museums and galleries that line the Mall.

74

Mobile in the Central Court of the East Building, National Gallery of Art. Natural interior air currents gently propel this mobile designed by Alexander Calder. The mobile, 29 feet high by 70 feet wide, was patterned after a small mobile Calder made just before he died.

75

Henry Moore statue, East Building of the National Gallery. This work by the British sculptor Henry Moore is entitled "Knife Edge Mirror Two Piece." It is an enlarged mirror image of a sculpture he designed in 1962 for a London Park. The work is in two pieces with a total weight of approximately 15 tons.

76

The Capitol from the roof of the East Building of the National Gallery of Art.

77

Reflection in the steel sculpture on the plaza of the Air and Space Museum.

78-79

The National Gallery of Art. In the 1930s, industrialist and statesman Andrew Mellon bequeathed his collection of Old Masters to the United States. In addition he provided $15 million to build the gallery that houses them. By his own request, the building was not named after him to encourage other art collectors to make donations as well. The gallery was designed by John Russell Pope.

80, 81

The Air and Space Museum. This marble, glass and steel museum has been called Washington's most American piece of public architecture. Here, the plane flown by the Wright brothers at Kitty Hawk, Charles Lindberg's Spirit of St. Louis, the Apollo 11 spacecraft, together with many other historic aircraft are on permanent exhibition. Several missiles and a DC-3 Dakota aircraft for the exhibit were so large that the museum was literally constructed around them. It is the city's most popular museum.

83

Smithsonian Institution. When James Smithson, an English scientist who never saw the United States, died in 1829, he left his entire fortune of $500,000 to the United States "to found at Washington, under the name of the Smithsonian Institution, an establishment for the increase and diffusion of knowledge among men." The Institution was formally established by an Act of Congress in 1846. Its first building, often called the "Red Castle on the Mall," was designed by James Renwick, a prominent architect of the day. Because its design did not conform to the classic architecture of other museums that had been built along the Mall, there was a move at one time to tear it down. It survived the threat and now houses administrative offices and the tomb of its founder.

Donations to the Institution range from aircraft to collections of political campaign buttons. Often known as "The Nation's Attic," the Smithsonian has more than 65 million catalogued objects in its collection.

84-85

Mormon Temple, Kensington, Maryland. This white marble structure rising out of a wooded hillside is the only Temple for Mormons east of the Mississippi River. The statue mounted on the highest spire represents the

Angel Moroni who is credited with revealing the Book of Mormon to Joseph Smith, founder of the Church of Jesus Christ of Latter Day Saints.

86, 87, 89

Cathedral Church of Sts. Peter and Paul. George Washington wanted the country to have a national church and selected Mount St. Alban, the highest hill in the city, as its site. Most of the stone carvings for the cathedral were prepared in workshops on the cathedral grounds, although some stones were carved after they were in place. Archways are illuminated by the light from a stained glass window.

90, 91

Arlington National Cemetery and the Honor Guard at the Tomb of the Unknown Soldier. The Tomb of the Unknown Soldier was established in 1921 for a "soldier known but to God" who died in World War I. Later, unknowns of World War II and of the Korean War were interred here. Arlington Cemetery was once the home of General Robert E. Lee, but was converted to a burial ground for war dead during the Civil War. There are two presidents buried here, William Howard Taft and John F. Kennedy. Major Pierre L'Enfant who planned the layout of City of Washington is buried just off the portico of Custis-Lee Mansion at a point commanding a superb view of the city he designed.

92

Arlington National Cemetery. There are more than 185,000 people buried here. Although grander headstones mark the graves of distinguished Americans, the ordinary soldiers' and sailors' graves are marked by small identical stones in survey-perfect lines. Graves are now restricted to those who have served honorably in the nation's military, but there are sections of the cemetery that hold the graves of former slaves. One memorial holds the remains of 2,111 unknown soldiers from the Civil War Battle of Bull Run.

93

Adams Monument in Rock Creek Cemetery. Henry Adams, author, historian, and grandson of John Quincy Adams, commissioned Augustus Saint-Gaudens, the country's leading sculptor in the late nineteenth century, to create a memorial to his wife, Marian. Set in a small enclosure, the six foot, genderless figure has been called by many names, among them, The Mystery of the Hereafter, Nirvana, The Peace of God and Grief. The figure untitled by the sculptor, evokes a sense of peace as it stares forever downward. John Hay, a close friend of Adams, wrote that the statue suggests "infinite wisdom, a past without beginning and a future without end, a repose after limitless experience, a peace to which nothing matters." During his lifetime, Adams often came to contemplate the memorial, as did Eleanor Roosevelt when the burdens of her position became too great.

94, 95

Columbus Fountain in front of Union Station. Lorado Taft's large fountain celebrates Christopher Columbus' discovery of the new world. A 15-foot statue of Columbus stands behind a greatly modified ship's prow with a figurehead symbolizing the Spirit of Discovery. The ship serves as a pedestal for the statue which is carved from a single block of white marble. The artist, drawing on the simplicity of Egyptian sculptures, wished to suggest calm and permanency.

96, 97

Georgetown. A busy tobacco trading port on the Potomac long before the creation of the District of Columbia, Georgetown today has an active and crowded business district adjacent to an area of elegant Federal period homes. Since it is one of the oldest communities in North America, any alteration to building facades is subject to the scrutiny of preservationist interests.

98

Residential area of Capitol Hill. Narrow three-story row houses were built at the turn of the century to house the growing number of civil servants. Today's public employees are largely responsible for the restoration of many of these old homes to their former beauty.

100-101

The Pension Building. Built after the Civil War for offices concerned with dispensing soldiers' pension checks, this majestically proportioned hall has been the site of a number of inaugural balls. Major General Montgomery Meigs, who served as Lincoln's Quartermaster General, designed the building.

103

A Metro station. Designers of the Washington Metro stations believed that a sense of dignity should prevail underground as well as above. Therefore, they chose an indirectly lighted, vaulted tunnel as their station design. The planners hoped to avoid one modern problem — graffiti — by having passengers board and leave trains from a center island.

104

Towpath along the C & O Canal. The canal that was to make Washington a commercial center is today a National Park, extending from Georgetown to the Cumberland Gap. The towpath was used by the horses and mules and their tenders while towing barges up and down the canal. The average round trip for a barge was eight days, four-and-a-half days with the barge loaded, three-and-a-half with it empty.

105

Fletcher's Boat House. Located above Georgetown on the Washington side of the Potomac, this boat house supplies many of the canoes and other boats used for recreation on the Potomac.

106-107

Central Washington. The federal city is an atypically "lowrise" city because of height restrictions instituted to be sure that buildings did not overshadow the majesty of the Capitol.

108

Theodore Roosevelt Island. The site of an eighteenth-century estate, this island in the Potomac is now a wildlife refuge in honor of the former president who was known as a conservationist. There is no vehicular traffic on the island, which is reached by way of a footbridge from the Virginia side of the Potomac.

109

An early-morning sculler. Sculling is a popular sport in the Washington area, and the Potomac a favorite practice area. Over the years, a number of the teams from the area have been of championship caliber.

111

Washington Monument. Fourth of July fireworks attract large crowds to the Mall. From the Capitol to the Iwo Jima Memorial, area residents and visitors alike crowd into their favorite vantage points to view the celebration. The usual display involves launching some 2000 projectiles containing about 1000 pounds of explosives over a period of a half-hour.

118-119

A time exposure of Metrobus lights through the windows of the Forrestal Building. Washington continues to grow and reflect the tastes and needs of the country. It no longer looks so often to the past for inspiration and direction, but it remains on easy terms with history.

THE QUOTATIONS

15
Captain John Smith to his crew, 1609

24
Thomas Jefferson, Letter to Samuel Kercheval, 1816, inscription on the Jefferson Memorial

29
Nathaniel Hawthorne, *Twice-Told Tales*, 1837

35
William Howard Taft, 1909-1913

43
Thomas Paine, *The Rights of Man*, II

45
Frederick Douglass, in *Washington in the New Era 1870-1970*, p. 14

50
Carl Sandburg, *Slabs of the Sunburnt West*, "Washington Monument at Night," 1922

65
Alfred, Lord Tennyson, "Palace of Art," 1873

73
Walter Pater, *The Renaissance*, 1873

80
Amelia Earhart Putnam, *Courage*

82
Albert Einstein, inscription on statue by Robert Berks, on Constitution Avenue

88
W.H. Auden, *On This Island*, "Look, stranger, on this island now," 1937

93
Aeschylus, *Agamemnon*, 525-456 B.C.

110
John Adams, 1800